THE FOLLOWING ENDORSEMENTS REPRESENT only a few of the people who invested their time and knowledge in the creation of this book. Some have entries in the book as well as many others who also contributed to the research, accuracy, and completion of this tool and resource.

### Mentor to the Author – Batya Shufrin

I am a born-again Jew that has been a part of Messianic Judaism for over 20 years. Although I was born and raised in the United States, I have also lived in several cities in Israel over the years. It has truly been a joy to mentor Julie for the last two and a half years in her quest for knowledge as she embraced the true roots of our Christian faith. It was my pleasure contributing to the accuracy and cultural guidance in the creation of *I Am Newish Jewish*.

Julie has exhibited great enthusiasm and hunger to learn as well as pass on to others the knowledge that she has acquired. That was, and is, the reason for this book. What started out as her personal notes have been transformed into a learning tool and resource for others.

### Mainstream Christian Convert to the Messianic Movement – Colby Hudson

My biblical foundation, just like Julie, is rooted in a Baptist church. In 2012, the Lord guided me to a messianic fellowship where I was introduced to the Hebrew roots of our Christian faith. My attempt to acquire knowledge about Messianic Christianity would have been greatly accelerated if I had access to the *I Am Newish Jewish* book. I highly recommend this valuable resource that clearly explains how the biblical feasts Jewish holidays are to be celebrated.

**Author's note:** Colby contributed to the design layout and the accuracy of the biblical and cultural information contained in *I Am Newish Jewish*.

### Messianic Bible Teacher and Ministry Leader - Matthew Shaw

Matthew is a Messianic Jew, born in the United States, lived in Israel, then South Africa and attended a Messianic Fellowship there. While in Israel and thereafter, he acquired education and knowledge of the culture, language, and customs. Sharing his wisdom with Julie sparked a passion for the biblical feasts and traditions, as well as a different way of life.

Matthew states, "Come along with Julie in her journey of discovering the great riches the Almighty of Israel has bestowed upon His people in every generation. *I Am Newish Jewish* is a tool to learn of the basics of the biblical feasts and holidays whether a beginner or as a refresher of the knowledge, respect, and beauty of these historical events."

# I AM NEWISH JEWISH

## A New Testament Perspective of the Biblical Feasts and Holidays

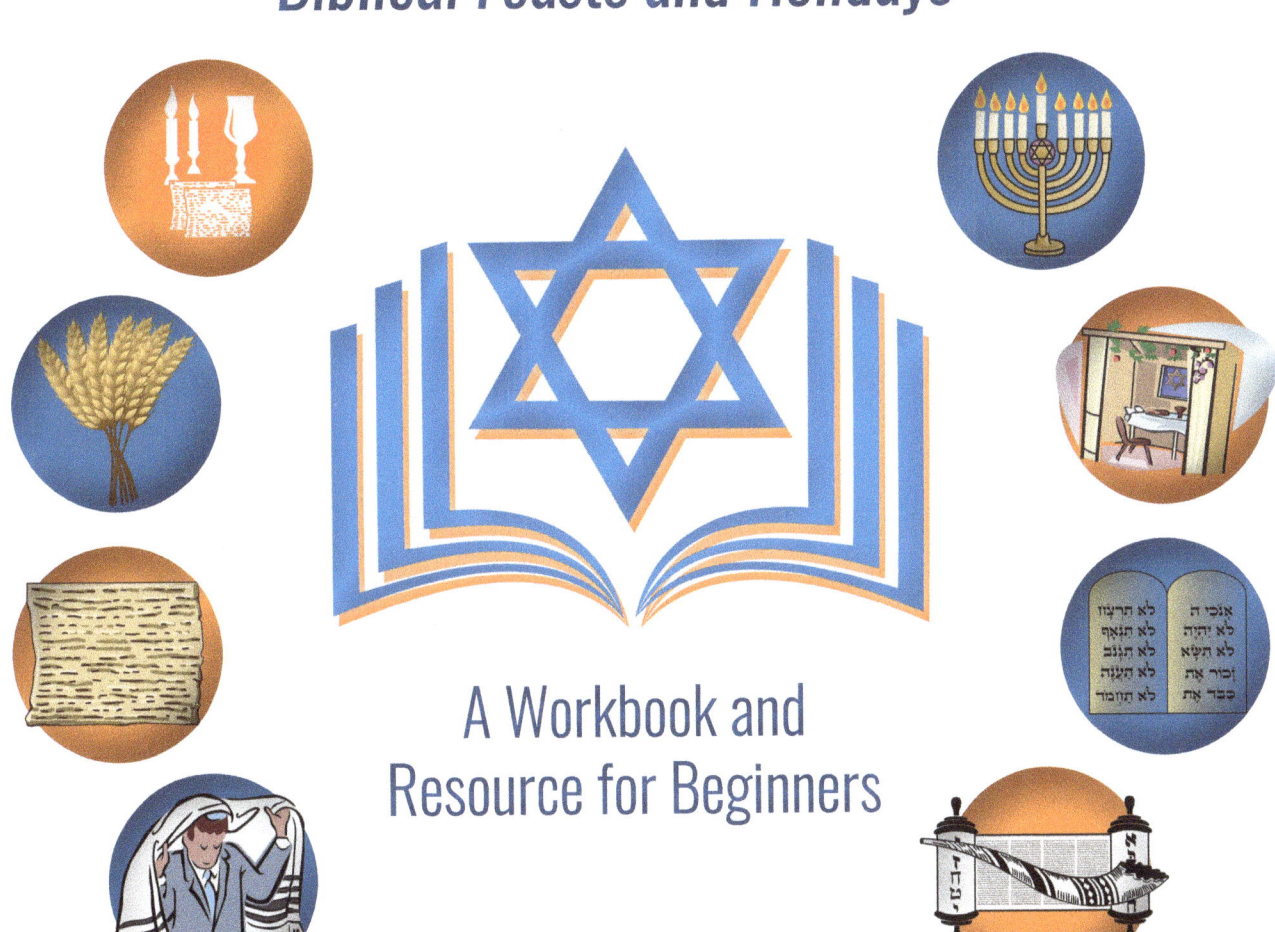

### A Workbook and Resource for Beginners

## Julie Caliendo

Published by Moedim Publications | Mesa, Arizona | 2022

Published by Moedim Publications

**SECOND EDITION**

*I Am Newish Jewish, A New Testament Perspective
of the Biblical Feasts and Holidays*

Copyright © 2022 Julie Caliendo

Cover & book interior design by
Multimedia Publishing Project
MultimediaPublishingProject.com | 480-939-9689

Cover artwork by Chris Moore

Paperback ISBN: 979-8-9852981-1-6

Library of Congress Control Number: 2022949548

Scripture quotations taken from the (NASB®) New
American Standard Bible®, Copyright © 1995 by
The Lockman Foundation. Used by permission.
All rights reserved. www.lockman.org.

Printed in the United States of America.

# Dedication

**T**O MY SON, DANIEL: I write as a legacy of love to you. It is my prayer that you will grow in the knowledge and wisdom of God's love and His plans for your life.

This study of the Word is also dedicated to our Congregational Leaders of this amazing ministry: Kane and Christine Adkins, Son of David Messianic Fellowship. I believe in giving recognition where it is due. A simple thank you seems inadequate to express my heartfelt gratitude to them for inspiring and supporting my relentless quest for the truth. They have both patiently mentored me by answering my hundreds of questions. Some may call them pastors or rabbis, I call them family. It has been a blessing becoming a part of their family and lives sharing a mutual passion for Christ by walking in God's truth.

# Contents

I Am Newish Jewish "Theme Verses" . . . . . . . . . . . . . . . . . . . . . . . . . . . . . . . . ix

Be a disciple. Make a disciple. Change the world. . . . . . . . . . . . . . . . . . xi

Acknowledgements . . . . . . . . . . . . . . . . . . . . . . . . . . . . . . . . . . . . . . . . . .xiii

Preface . . . . . . . . . . . . . . . . . . . . . . . . . . . . . . . . . . . . . . . . . . . . . . . . . . . xv

Introduction - The Author's Journey Begins . . . . . . . . . . . . . . . . . . . . . xvii

What We Believe, The Foundation . . . . . . . . . . . . . . . . . . . . . . . . . . . . . xxi

Understanding the Terminology . . . . . . . . . . . . . . . . . . . . . . . . . . . . . . .xxiii

Feasts, High Holy Days and Holidays . . . . . . . . . . . . . . . . . . . . . . . . . . . . 1

    Rosh Chodesh, New Moon – Monthly . . . . . . . . . . . . . . . . . . . . . . . . . 2

    The High Holy Days . . . . . . . . . . . . . . . . . . . . . . . . . . . . . . . . . . . . . . . 3

    Overview of Event Calendar . . . . . . . . . . . . . . . . . . . . . . . . . . . . . . . . . 5

    Tisha B'Av – Optional Participation . . . . . . . . . . . . . . . . . . . . . . . . . . . 8

Messianic Seal of Israel . . . . . . . . . . . . . . . . . . . . . . . . . . . . . . . . . . . . . . . 9

The Messianic Feasts and Celebrations . . . . . . . . . . . . . . . . . . . . . . . . . . 11

    Celebration of Purim, Lots – Spring Event . . . . . . . . . . . . . . . . . . . . 12

    Pesach, Passover – Spring Event. . . . . . . . . . . . . . . . . . . . . . . . . . . . 14

Chag HaMatzot, Feast of Unleavened Bread – Spring Event . . . . . . . . . . 16

Feast of First Fruits – Spring Event . . . . . . . . . . . . . . . . . . . . . . . . . . . . . . 17

Shavuot, Feast of Weeks, Pentecost – Spring Event . . . . . . . . . . . . . . . . . 18

Feast of Trumpets (New Year) – Yom Teruah
(Rosh Hashanah) – Fall Event . . . . . . . . . . . . . . . . . . . . . . . . . . . . . . . . . . 20

Yom Kippur, Day of Atonement – Fall Event . . . . . . . . . . . . . . . . . . . . . . . 22

Sukkot, Feast of Tabernacles – Fall Event . . . . . . . . . . . . . . . . . . . . . . . . . 24

Shemini Atzeret, Feast of Tabernacles (last day) – Fall Event . . . . . . . . . 26

Simchat Torah, Rejoicing with/of the Torah – Fall Event . . . . . . . . . . . . . 27

Hanukkah, Feast of Dedication – Winter Event . . . . . . . . . . . . . . . . . . . . . 28

## Resources for Further Learning . . . . . . . . . . . . . . . . . . . . . . . . . . . . . . . 31

The Biblical Calendar . . . . . . . . . . . . . . . . . . . . . . . . . . . . . . . . . . . . . . . . . . 32

The Biblical Day . . . . . . . . . . . . . . . . . . . . . . . . . . . . . . . . . . . . . . . . . . . . . . 33

Hebrew Days of the Week . . . . . . . . . . . . . . . . . . . . . . . . . . . . . . . . . . . . . . 34

Resources for Research . . . . . . . . . . . . . . . . . . . . . . . . . . . . . . . . . . . . . . . . 35

Contact Us . . . . . . . . . . . . . . . . . . . . . . . . . . . . . . . . . . . . . . . . . . . . . . . . . . 37

## About the Author . . . . . . . . . . . . . . . . . . . . . . . . . . . . . . . . . . . . . . . . . . . . 39

## The Stained-Glass Cross Logo . . . . . . . . . . . . . . . . . . . . . . . . . . . . . . . . . 41

Portrait by the Master . . . . . . . . . . . . . . . . . . . . . . . . . . . . . . . . . . . . . . . . . 42

## Also by Julie Caliendo . . . . . . . . . . . . . . . . . . . . . . . . . . . . . . . . . . . . . . . . 44

# I Am Newish Jewish "Theme Verses"

### Numbers 6:24-26 NASB

"The LORD bless you and keep you;
The LORD make his face shine on you,
And be gracious to you;
The LORD lift up His countenance on you,
And give you peace."

### II Timothy 2:15 KJV

Study to show thyself approved unto God,
a workman that needeth not to be ashamed,
rightly dividing the word of truth.

# Be a disciple. Make a disciple. Change the world.

**W**HY LEARN ABOUT THE HEBREW ROOTS OF THE CHRISTIAN FAITH? Why study the feasts of the Lord? Why should we keep the Sabbath? Does God care what we eat?

The answers to these questions, and so many more, are of no benefit if we do not cultivate a personal relationship with the Savior of the world. He was there with His Father at creation and personally interpreted the Torah to give us a full understanding of what it means to love the Lord our God with all of our soul, mind and strength, and to love our neighbors as ourselves.

To be disciples, we must first acknowledge our separation from God as a result of sin, repent of that sin and forsake it, and believe in the saving work of the Lord Yeshua HaMashiach (Jesus Christ). We are saved by grace through faith in Him alone, and not by any works of our own. Rather, we are saved TO DO good works, TO KEEP His appointed times and TO LEARN to keep His laws to the best of our ability. His perfect Torah spells out how believers are to pursue justice and mercy, and to shine with the good news of salvation to those who have no hope.

There is great joy in the presence of the angels of God over one sinner who repents. First, come to know your Savior and King - and the joy of His salvation - and then ask what is commanded of you, for those who love Him obey His commandments.

Let us invite Father, Son and Holy Spirit into your reading about His Word and His ways. Say the following prayer with great expectations of what He is about to do in your life. If you have prayed it before this moment, then invite His presence into every word. If this is your first time opening your heart and mind to receive Yeshua into your life then embrace your commitment to a new life in Christ. Say it also, if you are renewing your promise to follow Him. It's a win-win experience.

"God, Adonai, I know I am a sinner and I am sorry for the sins I have committed. I know my sins put distance between us and I know I cannot save myself. Only Your Son, Yeshua, can save me and eliminate the distance between us. I believe Yeshua is Your Son, who died on a cross for my sins and rose from the dead. I receive Him as my Savior and Messiah. I accept your offer of forgiveness and everlasting life. Thank you, Father. In the Name of Yeshua I pray. Amen."

Whatever your experience, if you have questions about what it means to be saved, please know we are here to answer your questions and walk this journey with you. You are not alone. Welcome to the Kingdom!

Blessings in Yeshua,

*Kane and Christine Adkins*

# Acknowledgements

ASPECIAL THANK YOU TO Kane and Christine Adkins, Batya Shufrin, Colby Hudson, Matthew Shaw, Lillian Ferola, and Julaine Stark. They walked with me on this journey to acquire the knowledge of God's Word from both the Christian and Jewish perspectives. We all share a mutual passion for truth, God's truth.

The Jewish symbols used to designate the feasts and holidays were created by an amazing graphic artist, Chris Moore. He is very knowledgeable about the Messianic beliefs and art and designed them with this book in mind. He is a great encourager of the faith and also contributed to the contents of this writing.

# Preface

**T**HIS INFORMATION WAS COMPILED FOR THOSE FEELING THE CALL from traditional Christian church congregations into Messianic fellowships. I started to write a one or two-page fact sheet during services as a reference tool. I was so excited by all the information, almost overwhelmed, that I was forced to expand my original concept into this book. It turned out to be a much greater endeavor than I imagined. I was getting confused so I decided to get organized and get smart. I am providing you with a basic overview that I wish I'd had as a reference tool, before my curious mind led me on this amazing life-changing journey. It is meant to be inspirational and educational.

To verify information provided here, I researched not only authoritative Hebrew/Jewish websites (public domain), books and other materials, I also consulted extensively experienced pastors, Messianic leaders, and other knowledgeable individuals. Although I am relatively new to this field of study, I want to be as accurate, yet concise as possible, about conveying what I have learned. Just as mainstream churches have variations in practices, even within the same denomination, so do various Messianic fellowships. The common ground is that they all have the same foundational belief that Yeshua is the Messiah. What knowledge I acquired through this research was a major part of my decision to follow this way of life.

Each of the events and feasts mentioned here are far more complex than I could explain in this concise explanation. Many books have been published on each of the feasts individually, but I only gave them a page or two of explanation as an overview and brief reference tool. Please keep in mind, I am still under construction. God is teaching me something new and wonderful every day. The more I read the scriptures, the more He reveals its meaning to me.

# Introduction - The Author's Journey Begins

**M**Y JOURNEY INTO MESSIANIC JUDAISM STARTED IN AUGUST 2019. I was raised in traditional Christian churches, grew up with the Bible and have been a committed Christian for many decades. I ventured into an expansion of my Christian beliefs when I started attending Son of David Messianic Fellowship. I opened my mind and proceeded prayerfully and carefully. So glad I did.

I have been a believer in Jesus Christ as my savior and Messiah for over fifty years. My quest into the Messianic beliefs began by visiting a church service out of curiosity. These new studies allowed me to truly embrace my biblical roots for the first time. I have been on this journey for almost three years. What an adventure! What a ride!

What is "Messianic," you ask? The Messianic movement seeks a return to the Hebrew roots of mainstream Christianity, combined with elements of modern Judaism. The cornerstone of our faith is Yeshua HaMashiach (Jesus the Messiah). He descended from the tribe of Judah, through the royal line of David, and fulfilled the prophecies regarding the salvation of Israel and the restoration of relationship between God and man. Everything I have expressed here is verifiable in God's Word. The foundation of Christian beliefs is found in the first five books of the Bible:

Genesis, Exodus, Leviticus, Numbers and Deuteronomy. These are also known as: "The Books of the Law," "The Books of Moses" or the "Torah." Messianic Jews are often people who are Jewish by birth and come to a belief in Yeshua/Jesus as their Messiah. Then they consider themselves "completed" Jews or Messianic Jews. The Messianic movement also includes non-Jewish Christians who have been grafted into Israel through the blood of Christ.

This was my first exposure to the Hebraic foundation of the Bible that I grew up with in the Baptist and Pentecostal churches. I found these studies of my Hebraic roots linked with Christianity both captivating and overwhelming. I have read the Bible through several times, each journey in a different version: King James, New King James, New International, New Living Translation. I recently finished reading the Complete Jewish Study Bible (Messianic) as part of my quest for knowledge and understanding. How did I miss this rich culture, history and religious practice all these years? I looked at this book for the first time through the eyes of a Jewish Jesus: His ancestry, prophecies and fulfillment, and was able to connect both the Old and New Testament to completion.

The mainstream Christian churches I attended never focused on the Old Testament or Torah portion of the Bible, they only pulled scriptures out of context to suit their sermons. It's dangerous to take scripture out of context. It may give an untruthful twist to the truth. They are not considering the whole story. No wonder why I never saw the big picture!

I remember saying to myself as a child, "Someday I'm going to go to the Holy Land (Israel) and see all this for myself. I want to walk where Jesus walked." In 2017 my dream came true when I toured Israel on a life-changing adventure into the past, present and future. I thought I was already immersed in biblical history, but I did not comprehend the long-term ramifications of this trip. It birthed a new perspective that is still resonating. What a paradigm shift!

I have always been curious about what the people called "Jewish Christians" believe, even more so after my trip to Israel, but never ventured into one of their services. My Pentecostal church in Chandler, Arizona announced that we were adding a Messianic Fellowship at our location with services on Saturdays. I thought it was strange to worship on Saturdays, hmmm.... I was now presented with the opportunity to expand the borders of my church "tent" and finally attend a center of worship that was based on both Christ and his Hebrew identity.

From the first meeting with the Fellowship, I felt I had come home and that was where I belonged. At that moment, when I met Congregational Leaders: Kane Adkins, his amazing wife Christine, and their five children, I was compelled to attend. I knew God was calling me in this new direction. Saturday is the Lord's Sabbath, but I have been a Pentecostal and part of the Assemblies of God Church worshiping on Sundays for over forty years. God is not leading me to leave one to join the other, but simply to expand. Therefore, I am now Messianic Newish Jewish on Saturdays and Pentecostal on Sundays.  Oy vey and praise the Lord!

I was eager to learn, so I attended almost every service, feast, and celebration, but there was still so much information I didn't understand. I was like a sponge soaking it all up in on-the-job training. Although Kane, a passionate teacher, presented the tools I needed, I found it overwhelming to comprehend and retain it all. I took copious notes at every meeting. As a retired instructional designer and banker by trade, I think in terms of details: organization, structure, and resources for further training. Although I am not Jewish by birth, I know that I have been grafted into the family of God by the blood of Christ. This book is my gift to others who are "Newish Jewish," just like me. I invite you to come and grow with me.

This overview serves as a tool, not a comprehensive study on each subject. It started out as a one-page cheat sheet per feast and has developed into this book. What a shocker! This wealth of information could not be contained in one simple page per topic. To facilitate your Judaic quest for knowledge, in the last section of this book I have provided several pages of resources to further your studies. For your convenience, this workbook contains several lines to add your own notes, where space allowed.

At this point in time, I don't pretend to have everything figured out, in fact, I intend to seek His will and the truth of His Word the rest of my days. I am always happy to accept new information to build my knowledge base and expand what information I have gathered so far. I will continue to acquire truth in the midst of a multitude of confusion and false teaching. Please be patient, God's not finished with me yet, or you.

I hope this beginner's endeavor will inspire you to enhance your own knowledge base. It is my prayer that you will springboard beyond this book into all of God's truth.

Enjoy your journey,

*Reverend Julie Caliendo*

# What We Believe, The Foundation

## THE SCRIPTURES

We believe that the Scriptures, consisting of the Torah, Prophets, Writings, all three of which are often referred to as the "Old Testament," and the Apostolic Scriptures, also referred to as the "New Testament", are without error, being given by God to man through the Holy Spirit. The Scriptures are God's complete revelation of His plan of salvation for mankind, and they are the absolute, final authority for all matters of belief and practice.

## GOD AND YESHUA (JESUS)

We believe in one God, and in His Son, Yeshua the Messiah (Jesus), of whom the prophets of Israel spoke, conceived and born of the virgin Mary, "in whom all the fullness of deity dwells in bodily form, and who is the Word who became flesh and dwelt among us, and whose glory we beheld, the glory of the uniquely begotten Son of God, full of grace and truth." John 1:1-14; Colossians 2:9.

## THE HOLY SPIRIT (RUACH HAKODESH)

We believe that the Holy Spirit of God was sent as a comforter and teacher to indwell and regenerate those who believe, guiding and instructing them towards holiness and righteous living in accordance with God's Word.

## MANKIND

We believe that God created mankind (male and female) in His image, but that all of mankind has sinned and fallen short of God's glory. Romans 3:23

## SALVATION

We believe that God's Son, Yeshua, paid the substitutionary penalty of sin, unto death, for all who believe in Him and His work of salvation, which is the sole way for us to stand before God in righteousness. All who are saved through faith become part of God's covenant family and become new creations, indwelt by the Holy Spirit. Justification is only by faith through the grace of God and cannot be earned; obedience to the Torah is the pursuit of righteousness and an imitation of the character of God, not an attempt to earn salvation through individual merit.

## ISRAEL

We believe that both the nation of Israel, physically descended from Abraham, Isaac, and Jacob, and non-descendants of the nations will be blessed by the covenant with God if they accept the salvation offered through the Messiah, His Son.

## END TIMES

We believe that Yeshua will return one day to fulfill His plan for mankind, to rule and reign on the throne of David in Jerusalem, where the redeemed will visit the Temple for worship and the Word of the Lord will go forth from Zion.

# Understanding the Terminology

**M**Y FIRST CHALLENGE, IN THIS ENDEAVOR, WAS UNDERSTANDING the frequently confusing terminology and cultural definitions. As you will see by the definitions below, simple words have different meanings in Messianic life and culture. Pronouncing the Hebrew language is quite another challenge. I try not to embarrass myself with feeble attempts at speaking the language, but do so only with a few well-rehearsed cordialities. Understanding the following terminology will help your initial communication. I wish I would have been more informed about these things before I toured Israel.

## CHURCH NAMES

The Messianic "churches" are not called "churches" in Israel. They have labeled themselves as "Fellowship", "Community" or "Congregation." The reason for this is rooted in the governmental and rabbinical regulations, regarding the label of "church" in Israel, as opposed to a synagogue or temples.

## TIME FRAMES

Biblically, a "day" begins at sundown and carries over to sundown the next day, approximately twenty-four hours. Therefore, all the holidays begin at sundown on the first day and end at nightfall on the last day as shown on the calendar days of the designated event. Thus began the pattern for the marking of the days as noted in the Bible verse below:

**Genesis 1:3-5 -** Then God said, "Let there be light"; and there was light. And God saw the light, that it was good; and God divided the light from the darkness. God called the light Day, and the darkness He called Night. So the evening and the morning were the first day."

## MOED (SINGULAR) | MOEDIM (PLURAL)

A Hebrew word meaning "appointment" or "appointed time." Leviticus 23 contains references to God's appointed times. This word is sometimes translated as "holiday" or "festival" but is better understood as a divinely commanded appointment.

## FEASTS

There are "feasts", "celebrations", and "holy convocations." There are also "holidays" or "holy days" commemorating an event. These terms will be used frequently in this book and are often synonymous, but not always. Some were ordered by God and given to Moses (Moshe) to present to the people of Israel. Some of these are not commanded (mitzvot), they are considered tradition, such as Purim and Hanukkah. The Lord's feasts are listed in Leviticus 23.

## Notes – Things I want to remember

_____

_____

## SEASONS

The Lord's feasts are based on the agricultural calendar, which begins with Passover in the spring and ends with Sukkot in the fall. Much of their year is based on the planting and harvesting of barley, wheat, and grapes. The harvesting depends on when you plant it, spring or fall. I am a city girl, not familiar with farming. I have a lot to learn about this!

## GREETINGS

"Shalom" is often said as a hello and goodbye. It means "peace" in the sense of whole, complete, nothing missing or lacking, all inclusive. Other greetings are noted on the pages that explain each event.

## WORK VS NON-WORK DAYS

We are instructed not to work on specific days or events to set the time aside for rest. Examples: shopping, house cleaning, and other work must be done before sundown Friday (when Shabbat, the Sabbath, begins). Friday is also known as "preparation day" for the time of Shabbat. The other days, normal work is allowed. This is stated several times in Leviticus 23:8 "you shall not do any laborious work." NASB This statement is made in several verses in this chapter. The question arises so often: "Is this a work or no work day?"

## Notes – Things I want to remember

_____

_____

_____

_____

_____

# Feasts, High Holy Days and Holidays

# ROSH CHODESH, NEW MOON – MONTHLY

**I**T'S IMPORTANT TO HAVE A BASIC UNDERSTANDING of the calendar structure, including the "New Moon" cycles. It is the name for the first day of every month in the Hebrew calendar, marked by the birth of a new moon. It is considered a minor holiday. Today we use the Gregorian versus Hebrew lunisolar (Agricultural) Calendar. Feasts are dropped into the lunar cycle calendar so when you see a date mentioned in the Bible, keep in mind they are using the lunar version. Fasting and mourning are NOT allowed.

**Numbers 10:10 -** Also on the day of your gladness and in your appointed feasts, and on the first days of your months, you shall blow the trumpets over your burnt offerings, and over the sacrifices of your peace offerings; and they shall be as a reminder of you before your God. I am the LORD your God." NASB

## Notes – Things I want to remember

_____

_____

_____

_____

_____

_____

_____

_____

_____

**M**Y LIST BEGINS HIGH HOLY DAYS WITH SHABBAT followed by the spring and fall calendar sequence of feasts and holidays.

## Shabbat, Sabbath – Weekly

The Fourth Commandment is: "Remember the Sabbath day, to keep holy." Exodus 20:8. Let us grasp the importance of this holy time. I was never taught this kind of reverence. Also be mindful that Shabbat was created for man, not man for Shabbat.

> **Hebrew name:** Shabbat meaning Sabbath. The English word Sabbath came from the Hebrew meaning "to rest from labor;" the day of rest is used for the seventh day. (Exodus 16:23-26)
>
> **Pronunciation:** Sha-baht.
>
> On the seventh day you shall have a Sabbath of solemn rest. **No work! Exodus 35:2**

On the Hebrew calendar, Shabbat officially starts Friday at sunset, not when it gets dark. It ends on Saturday at sundown. Some Jews say it ends forty minutes up to two hours after sunset. Some say that it ends when three medium stars appear in the sky. Although there are variations, the point is to pray about it, make a decision and abide by it.

Genesis shows us that God created for six days and rested on the seventh. No work is done during this Sabbath timeframe. It is a day of rest.

**Purpose:** It is an intentional day of rest at the end of every week that is intended to provide space and time without work. The observer of this day is meant to find meaning and joy. It is the only holy day that originates with God's celebration of it and the commandment regarding the Sabbath is the fourth of the Ten Commandments: "Remember the Sabbath day, to keep it holy."

> **Leviticus 23:3 –** "For six days work may be done, but on the seventh day there is a Sabbath of complete rest, a holy convocation. You shall not do any work; it is a Sabbath to the Lord in all your dwellings." NASB

> **Exodus 20:8 –** "Remember the Sabbath day, to keep it holy." NASB

> **Isaiah 58:13-14 -** "If because of the sabbath, you turn your foot
> From doing your *own* pleasure on My holy day,
> And call the sabbath a delight, the holy *day* of the Lord honorable,
> And honor it, desisting from your own ways,
> From seeking your *own* pleasure
> And speaking *your own* word,
> Then you will take delight in the Lord,
> And I will make you ride on the heights of the earth;
> And I will feed you *with* the heritage of Jacob your father,
> For the mouth of the Lord has spoken." NASB

**Holiday Foods:** It is a time to enjoy foods you and your family love, plus some challah bread (a special egg bread). Make enough food in advance so that you don't have to work cooking lunch on Saturday! Friday should be used as a preparation day.

However it is observed, Shabbat is a great day to enjoy the time with family and friends, eat a lot, take walks, study Torah, sing songs, read stories to children, and take a nap or just chill out. The end of Shabbat is traditionally marked by a ritual called *Havdalah* during which songs are sung and blessings are said over wine/grape juice, spices, and light (a special twisted candle is used), separating Shabbat from the rest of the week.

**Shabbat Greeting:** Shabbat Shalom, which is Hebrew for peaceful Sabbath.

## Notes – Things I want to remember

_____

_____

# OVERVIEW OF EVENT CALENDAR

## (See next page)

**T**HE FOLLOWING CHART IS BASED ON THE GREGORIAN CALENDAR for biblical feasts to provide an overview of the sequence of events that can be adapted each year with new holiday dates. It notes the High Holy Days and their seasons. Reminder: The Lord's feasts are based on the agricultural calendar, therefore there is a continual annual rotation, just as the seasons of growth and life. Keep in mind, all Shabbats are counted as High Holy Days. All observances, except Passover, begin the prior evening.

These holy convocations are listed here in the calendar order of events, spring then fall. It is important to acknowledge the seasons because they indicate repetitive cycles.

The information here is based on the Jewish Hillel (pronounced Hi-lel) calendar. Purim and Hanukkah are NOT Appointed Times in the Torah, they are traditions; as such, not everyone celebrates them. Ask your congregation leaders which of the calendars they have chosen to follow.

**Note from the Author:** I found the multiple calendars to be very confusing, but I am still learning. I was advised to use the Hillel calendar. As you learn more in your quest for knowledge, add your own thoughts for future reference. I started this book by taking extensive notes as I was attending services and events. I enjoyed the journey so much it grew exponentially into this reference guide for me, as well as others.

## Notes – Things I want to remember

_____

_____

# SPRING FEAST CALENDAR SAMPLE

## Purim | Spring Tradition

Celebrates the defeat of the plot to destroy the Jews of Persia.
Esther 9:20-22

## Passover (Pesach) | Spring - High Holy Day

The deliverance of Israel from Egypt is remembered and is a Shabbat that leads into a seven-day feast period. It is a Shabbat day. Exodus 12:1-28

## First Fruits (Yom HaBikkurim) | Spring

The first-fruits was a sheaf of barley which was offered during the Feast of Unleavened Bread and is still observed today. The Scriptures say that First Fruits is the day after the weekly Sabbath. This aligns with Resurrection Day. Leviticus 23:9-11

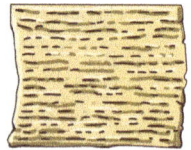

## Feast of Unleavened Bread (Chag HaMatzot) | Spring

During the seven-day festival no leaven (yeast) is eaten or possessed. The first and seventh days are **High Holy Days**. Leviticus 23:4-8

## Feast of Weeks (Shavuot) | Spring - High Holy Day

Commemorates the giving of the Law (Torah) at Mt. Sinai. It is a Shabbat day. Exodus 20:1-17

# FALL FEAST CALENDAR SAMPLE

• • • • • • • • • • • • • • • • • • •

### Feast of Trumpets (Yom Teruah) | Fall - High Holy Day
It is the first of the Jewish High Holy Days and the Jewish New Year (Rosh Hashanah). It starts the Ten Days of Penitence. It is a Shabbat day. Leviticus 23:23–32

### Day of Atonement (Yom Kippur) | Fall - High Holy Day
The most solemn day of the year that is devoted to fasting, prayer, and repentance. It is a Shabbat day. Leviticus 23:26–32, Matthew 27:32-50

### Feast of Tabernacles (Sukkot) | Fall - High Holy Day
Commemorates the dwelling of the Israelites in the wilderness. It is a Shabbat day. Leviticus 23:33-44

### Shemini Atzeret (Eighth Day of Assembly) | Fall (With Sukkot)
The eighth day of Sukkot. It is a Shabbat day. Leviticus 23:33-44

### Hanukkah (Feast of Dedication) | Winter Tradition
Is an eight-day holiday that celebrates the victory of the Maccabees over the Greeks, and the rededication of the temple in Jerusalem in 165 B.C.

## TISHA B'AV – OPTIONAL PARTICIPATION

**T**ISHA B'AV, THE FAST OF THE NINTH OF AV, is a day of mourning to commemorate the many tragedies that have befallen the Jewish people, many of which have occurred on the ninth of Av. It is a tradition, not a command. It occurs in July or August. For some, it is a day honored by volunteer fasting and prayer.

### Notes – Things I want to remember

# Messianic Seal of Israel

**T**HE THREE-PART INTERLOCKING INSIGNIA DESIGN consists of a menorah at the top, a Star of David in the middle and a fish (Greek: icthys) at the bottom. The star is created by joining the menorah base (upward triangle) with the top of the fish's tail (downward triangle).

When the triangles interlock, they form the six-point Star of David. This symbolically refers to the tri-unity of Abba Father's divine nature merging downwards from heaven as one with man in the earthly realm, who is created in His image and likeness. Yeshua is symbolized by the *fish* and Himself, claims to be the *root*. We see in the *Messianic Seal* that the *fish* is at the bottom of the *Seal* representing a strong foundation.

We have found that many people accept this as a symbol of Yeshua, others may not agree. This is presented here because it is so frequently seen in Israel, as well as around the world, that we felt it should be explained.

## Notes – Things I want to remember

# The Messianic Feasts and Celebrations

# CELEBRATION OF PURIM, LOTS – SPRING EVENT

**THE HEBREW NAME MEANS:** "Lots" because the villain cast lots to set the date for the Jews' destruction.

**PRONUNCIATION:** poor-im.

This is not a commanded festival of the Lord, it is a tradition.

There is no obligation to refrain from working. It is a **Work** day.

**Purpose:** This celebrates the defeat of the plot to destroy all the Jews in Persia. Read the Book of Esther for the whole story.

**THE FAST OF ESTHER** (*Taanit Esther*) is a dawn-to-nightfall fast held on the day before the joyous holiday of Purim. It commemorates the fasting of our ancestors in response to the dramatic chain of events that occurred during their exile in the Persian Empire. These events are recorded in the Book of Esther, and the salvation that came about at that time is celebrated on the holiday of Purim.

**Activities:** This is a fun celebration with food and fellowship, perhaps testimonies, and a brief teaching. The Bible is placed on a lectern or podium (or "bema" in a synagogue) and guests take turns reading a chapter to the audience until it is done. When Mordecai's name is read, they all cheer (the good guy), when Haman's name is said, they all boooo and stomp their feet! (the bad guy), but when the name of Esther is read, they all say "awwww." Biblical costumes can be worn, gifts may be given, noise makers can be used. I attended my first celebration last year and it was wonderful. We partnered with another messianic fellowship so I got to make new friends, too.

**Holiday Foods:** Triangular pastries called hamantashen (Haman's pockets), named for the bad guy in the Book of Esther. Some people also eat other foods with things hidden inside, like dumplings.

**Purim Greeting:** Happy Purim! You can say "Purim Sameah," which means "happy Purim."

## Notes – Things I want to remember

<br><br><br><br><br><br><br><br><br><br><br><br><br><br>

# PESACH, PASSOVER – SPRING EVENT

**HEBREW NAME MEANS:** *Pass over*.

**PRONUNCIATION:** Pe-sach

This Feast of the Lord is stated in Leviticus 23.

Because Pesach begins at twilight, there is no requirement to abstain from work before that time. However, most people take the day off work to prepare for the Seder meal event. It's a lot of work! Technically, Friday is a **work** day, but at sundown that stops as the Sabbath begins.

**Purpose:** Pesach was given to all of Israel. Traditionally, Passover and the Feast of Unleavened Bread are blended together to create an 8-day holiday to celebrate God freeing the Israelites from slavery in Egypt. The name refers to God's angel of death "passing over" the houses of the Israelites during the 10th plague, the killing of the first born.

Jesus fulfilled the Passover becoming our Passover lamb. The crucifixion happened as Israelite families were slaughtering and preparing lambs for their Passover meals. Activities: Preparations for the holiday week for heavily ritualized holiday meals, including the Seder, in which we are commanded to tell the story of Pesach every year. In their preparations, it is required that they remove all leaven from the home before the feast begins. (Refer to the Feast of Unleavened Bread page.) It is a tradition for a separate special set of dishes, pots and pans, glassware and utensils are used in kosher households during Pesach to ensure there is no contamination of leaven (yeast represents sin). It is the most celebrated Hebrew holiday in the world with distinctively unique foods and rituals – all delicious, all beautiful.

**Holiday Foods:** The biblical command for this feast says to eat unleavened bread for seven days and to remove all leaven from your home before the feast begins. This is the period where the Feast of Unleavened Bread traditionally overlaps with Pesach Seder. In our home, we get rid of anything leavened as well as any leavening agents. For the rest of the seven-day period, all meals and snacks do not contain any leavening agents or leavened products.

**About unleavened foods:** The following restrictions were commanded by God in the Torah, which apply to the native-born Israelites and Gentiles grafted in through faith. They eat no leavened bread or leavened food on Pesach, and instead eat matzah, which is unleavened bread (like a cracker or flatbread). There are many traditional foods that are eaten on Pesach, including matzah balls, gefilte fish, horseradish root and macaroons.

**Passover Greeting:** "Happy Pesach" or "Happy Passover." Some people say "Hag kasher v'sameach"—have a happy and kosher holiday.

## Notes – Things I want to remember

_____

_____

_____

_____

_____

_____

_____

# CHAG HAMATZOT, FEAST OF UNLEAVENED BREAD – SPRING EVENT

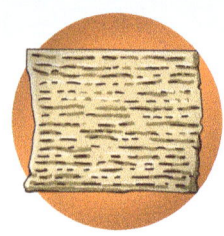

**HEBREW NAME MEANS:** feast of unleavened bread.

Also called "Feast of the Lord" in Leviticus 23:6-8.

**PRONUNCIATION:** Hag ha-mah-tzote. The Hag is (ch) using the guttural sound.

On the first and last day of the Feast of Unleavened Bread, there shall be no laborious work. **No work!** Leviticus 23

**Purpose:** The Feast of Unleavened Bread follows right after Pesach. Both Pesach and the Feast of Unleavened Bread are meaningful celebrations for Christians as we explore our Hebrew roots and grow in our faith. The meal for Pesach, called a *Seder*, isn't merely to nourish those who partake, but to serve as a memorial to what God did for His people in the Exodus from Egypt.

**Activities:** The Feast of Unleavened Bread is a seven-day feast. The first and last days are to be Sabbaths. These Sabbaths differ from the weekly Sabbath (Saturday) and may occur on any day of the week. Which day of the week they're on changes from year to year, but no matter what day they occur on, the same rules apply as for the weekly Sabbath – rest and keeping the day holy.

## Notes – Things I want to remember

_____

_____

_____

_____

## FEAST OF FIRST FRUITS – SPRING EVENT

Also known as "Feast of the Lord" in Leviticus 23:1-14.

There is no requirement to abstain from work. It is a **work** day.

The term "First Fruits" means there is more to come.

**Purpose:** Leviticus 23 states, First Fruits is the day after the Sabbath and occurs during the week of unleavened bread. There are different points of view on how it should be done. It is a ceremony performed which commences the marking off time to Shavuot or Pentecost (a countdown). The word "Pentecost" originates from the Greek term meaning "50 days."

The Torah teaches us that the priest was to wave the sheaves of grain from side to side with outstretched arms before the Lord (a wave offering). They would also perform a burnt offering, a meal offering and a drink offering. There is a prohibition against eating any *bread or* parched grain until the first fruits of the barley harvest were offered unto the Lord.

**Activities:** Because the Temple has been destroyed, the presentation of the loaves cannot be accomplished. In lieu of this, Messianic fellowships acknowledge this feast with a gathering and a meal. We can still eat, drink and be merry on this occasion until we have the third Temple.

## Notes – Things I want to remember

_____

_____

_____

# SHAVUOT, FEAST OF WEEKS, PENTECOST – SPRING EVENT

**PRONUNCIATION:** Shah-voo-oat

**HEBREW NAME MEANS:** Feast of Weeks – it is celebrated seven weeks after First Fruits.

Also known as "Feast of the Lord" or "Lord's Appointed Time." Leviticus 23:15-22

**AKA:** Christians refer to this occasion as Pentecost.

"You shall do no laborious work." **No work!**

**Purpose:** Shavuot marks the early summer grain/wheat harvest. Although not explicitly stated in the scripture, it is commonly held that the giving of Torah at Mt. Sinai occurred on Shavout. This marked the covenant between God and Israel (seven weeks after the Exodus from Egypt).

**Holiday Foods:** It's traditional to eat dairy foods on Shavuot, so lots of blintzes, cheese, and ice cream. (On "dairy holidays," people who keep kosher, according to rabbinical laws, do not eat meat.)

**Activities:** The Book of Ruth (a story about interfaith marriage and family!) is read in synagogues and some people participate in an all-night Torah study session, called Tikkun Leil Shavuot.

**Symbols of holiday:** Fruit, sheaves of wheat, and tablets (representing the giving of Torah).

**Greeting:** "Hag Sameah," which means "happy holiday" in Hebrew.

# Notes – Things I want to remember

# FEAST OF TRUMPETS (NEW YEAR) – YOM TERUAH (ROSH HASHANAH) – *FALL EVENT*

**Hebrew name means:** Feast of Trumpets. This term is often used interchangeably with Rosh Hashanah

Leviticus 23:23-25 - "You shall not do any laborious work." **No work!**

It is the first of the High Holy Days. Start of the Ten Days of Penitence (AKA: Ten Days of Awe).

**Purpose:** The trumpet (shofar) sounds to declare the coming of the King. It's the warning of the coming judgement. It's time to reflect and repent.

**Holiday Foods:** Apples and honey, round challah with raisins, honey cake, pomegranates, pumpkins and other round foods, sweet foods and foods that are gold-colored, like carrots.

**Activities:** Many Jews who don't go to synagogue the rest of the year, attend the marathon of synagogue services on Rosh Hashanah and Yom Kippur. One special activity that people don't want to miss is the sounding of the *shofar*, or ram's horn. Traditionally, people eat apples dipped in honey, to signify a sweet new year, and many people send New Year's cards.

The most important activity associated with this holiday time comes between Yom Teruah and Yom Kippur: trying to repair relationships and make apologies for bad behavior in the previous year.

**Symbols of Holiday:** The shofar or ram's horn, apples and honey, pomegranates, and the Book of Life.

**Greeting:** "Happy New Year" or *"Shanah Tovah."* If you want to give a more complete version of the greeting, try *"L'shanah tovah tikatevu,"* which means "May you be inscribed for a good year in the Book of Life."

## Notes – Things I want to remember

# YOM KIPPUR, DAY OF ATONEMENT – FALL EVENT

**HEBREW NAME MEANS:** Day of Atonement.

**PRONUNCIATION:** Yohm kee-poo.

**LEVITICUS 23:26-32 -** "You shall not do any laborious work." **No work!**

**Purpose:** The most solemn day of the year is devoted to fasting, prayer, and repentance. It is a day dedicated to fasting and is traditionally filled with prayer and collective confession and atonement. It is said that on Rosh HaShanah the Book of Life is written and on Yom Kippur it is sealed. Leviticus 16:29-30

**Holiday Foods:** None. It's a tradition to fast this day! No food. Children under age thirteen, women who are pregnant and those whose health might be harmed do not fast.

**Activities:** In addition to not eating, traditionally you would also not drink, not wash, not wear leather, nor have sexual relations. Many people go to synagogue for most of the day, and even those who are not observant may go for a special service called Yizkor, as an act of respect for the loved ones who have passed. The fast (and holiday) ends with a festive break-fast (breaking the fast) meal after sundown.

**Symbols of Holiday:** Shofar, people traditionally wear white clothing (symbolizing purity).

**Greeting:** "Have an easy fast" or *"Tsom Kal."* Some say *Shanah Tovah*, which is Hebrew for "Happy New Year" or *Gamar hatimah tovah,* "a good completion to your inscription in the Book of Life."

# Notes – Things I want to remember

# SUKKOT, FEAST OF TABERNACLES – FALL EVENT

**Hebrew name means:** Booths or tabernacles.

**Pronunciation:** Sue-coat

Also known as the "Feast of Booths"

There are **two non-work** days, the first day of Sukkot and the eighth day.

**Purpose:** Commemorates the dwelling of the Israelites in the wilderness. In ancient times when the Temple stood in Jerusalem, this was a pilgrimage holiday to celebrate the harvest. Rabbinic tradition now holds that this week-long holiday is when we remember the experience of the Israelites' years of wandering in the desert. Leviticus 23:33-43

**Holiday Foods:** No specific food, but fruit and vegetables are part of the harvest theme.

**Activities:** Families and communities build a sukkah (frequently referred to as a booth or hut) in the yard that will be used for the whole week of Sukkot for eating and entertaining. Some people even sleep in their sukkah (booth). These huts remind us of the ones our ancestors dwelled in while wandering in the desert. Rabbinic tradition holds that the sukkah should have three sides and a roof, but still be open to the elements. Leviticus 23:42

**Symbols of Holiday:** The sukkah, the lulav (a palm frond) and the etrog (a yellow citron or Citrus medica) used in the ritual to celebrate bounty. Also, a myrtle tree branch and a willow tree branch.

**Greeting:** Hag Sukkot Sameach (happy holiday in Hebrew) is the proper greeting for the first and last days of holiday, whereas the proper greeting for the intermediate days is Moedim l'simcha, which means "festivals for joy."

## Notes – Things I want to remember

_____

_____

_____

_____

_____

_____

_____

_____

_____

_____

_____

_____

_____

_____

_____

## SHEMINI ATZERET, FEAST OF TABERNACLES (LAST DAY) – FALL EVENT

Also known as Hoshana Rabbah

This is the last day of Sukkot, it is not its own event, it is part of Sukkot. This eighth day is a **do not work** day.

**HEBREW NAME SHEMINI MEANS:** eighth. It is the Eighth Day of Assembly of the Feast of Tabernacles. Atzeret means assembly with the root word atzor meaning tarry.

**Purpose:** It is a one-day holiday that immediately follows after the seventh day of Sukkot. This day is noted in John 7:37-39 - Now on the last day, the great *day* of the feast, Jesus stood and cried out, saying, "If anyone is thirsty, let him come to Me and drink. [38] The one who believes in Me, as the Scripture said, From his innermost being will flow rivers of living water.'" [39] But this He said in reference to the Spirit, whom those who believed in Him were to receive; for the Spirit was not yet *given*, because Jesus was not yet glorified.

**Activities:** It is a time when prayers or celebrations are made for rain and a good harvest for the coming year in the Hebrew calendar.

**Greeting:** No specific greetings for Shimini Atzaret or Simchat Torah.

### Notes – Things I want to remember

_____

_____

_____

## SIMCHAT TORAH, REJOICING WITH/OF THE TORAH – FALL EVENT

**Hebrew name means:** "Rejoicing in the Torah."

**Pronunciation:** The ch in Simchat is guttural.

This is not a commanded biblical festival. It initiates the new cycle of the Torah reading, therefore it is a celebration of the new beginning. There are no restrictions regarding **work**.

**Purpose:** It celebrates the end of the year cycle of reading the Torah portion and starting it anew for the new year. This is also a day of praying for early rains in the country.

**Holiday Foods:** No specific food.

**Activities:** Simchat Torah denotes the finishing the annual cycle of Torah reading. The very last words of the Torah are read. As soon as we finish the Torah, we start reading it over from the beginning again. The gathering is punctuated by the blowing of the shofar and congregational dancing with the Torah scrolls.

**Symbols of Holiday:** The Torah scroll, flags the children carry, dancing.

**Greeting:** Hag sameah (happy holiday in Hebrew).

### Notes – Things I want to remember

_____

_____

_____

# HANUKKAH, FEAST OF DEDICATION – WINTER EVENT

**Hebrew name means:** Dedication.

**Pronunciation:** It's the spelling on this one that will throw you – Chanukah, Chanukkah, Hanukkah, Hanuka – they're all right – it's a transliteration of the Hebrew, so you can't spell it wrong!

Also known as Festival of Lights

There is no requirement to abstain from **work**.

Hanukkah is not commanded, it is a tradition.

**Purpose:** Hanukkah is an eight-day holiday that commemorates the Jewish recapture and rededication of the Temple in Jerusalem in 164 BCE. It is referred to in John 10:22. Yeshua went up to Jerusalem to celebrate the Feast of Dedication.

**Holiday Foods:** Fried foods, especially potato pancakes, called latkes, and jelly doughnuts called sufganiyot. We eat foods fried in oil to remind us of the small amount of oil (just enough for one day) that miraculously burned for eight days when the Jews rededicated the Temple.

**Activities:** The main observance is lighting the menorah candles in a ceremonial lamp formally called a Hanukkiah, or commonly labeled a Hanukkah menorah, each night for 8 nights. Playing with a top called a dreidel is another fun tradition. Hanukkah is considered a "minor festival."

**Symbols of Jewish holiday:** Hanukkiah, candles, and dreidel.

**Hanukkah Greeting:** Chag Hanukkah Samech (happy Hanukkah!) or Chag Urim Sameach (happy festival of lights).

## Hanukkah Menorah / Hanukkiah

LIGHTING A SPECIAL, NINE-BRANCHED CANDELABRUM is the main ritual on Hanukkah. With nine branches, it is lit each night to celebrate the miracle of oil lasting eight days. The ninth candle is called the *Shamash* and is used to light all the others. Most people — including Jews — incorrectly refer to this as a Menorah, when in fact the correct name for the candleholder is Hanukkiah or Hanukkah Menorah.

According to strict Jewish law, a Hanukkiah should have eight candleholders of the same height and a ninth branch that is set higher than the rest. Olive oil was traditionally used to light the Hanukkiah, later replaced by candles that are inserted incrementally each night from right to left, but lit from left to right. Since 1998, the world's largest Hanukkiah — a 32-ft.-high, gold-colored steel structure — can be found during the Festival of Lights in New York City's Central Park.

## Menorah

A MENORAH, WHICH HAS ONLY SEVEN CANDLEHOLDERS, was the lamp used in the ancient holy temple in Jerusalem — now a symbol of Judaism and an emblem of Israel.

## Notes – Things I want to remember

_____

_____

_____

_____

_____

# Notes – Things I want to remember

# Resources for Further Learning

# THE BIBLICAL CALENDAR

**T**HE FOLLOWING IS THE BASIC INFORMATION about the two kinds of calendars used:

**Civil Calendar -** Official calendar of kings, childbirth, and contracts

**Religious (Sacred) Calendar -** From which festivals are computed.

The Hebrew months were alternately 30 and 29 days long. Their year is shorter than ours at 354 days. Therefore, about every three years (7 times in 19 years) and extra 29- day month Veadar was added between Adar and Nisan.

| Civil Calendar | | | Religious Calendar | | |
|---|---|---|---|---|---|
| GENESIS 1-EXODUS 12 | | | EXODUS 12 | | |
| 1. | Tishrei | Sep | 1. | Nisan (Aviv) | Mar |
| 2. | Cheshvan | Oct | 2. | Iyar | Apr |
| 3. | Kislev | Nov | 3. | Sivan | May |
| 4. | Tevet | Dec | 4. | Tammuz | Jun |
| 5. | Shevat | Jan | 5. | Av | Jul |
| 6. | Adar | Feb | 6. | Elul | Aug |
| 7. | Nisan (Aviv) | Mar | 7. | Tishrei | Sep |
| 8. | Iyar | Apr | 8. | Cheshvan | Oct |
| 9. | Sivan | May | 9. | Kislev | Nov |
| 10. | Tammuz | Jun | 10. | Tevet | Dec |
| 11. | Av | Jul | 11. | Shevat | Jan |
| 12. | Elul | Aug | 12. | Adar | Feb |

## Notes – Things I want to remember

_____

_____

# THE BIBLICAL DAY

**The Biblical Day** is from sunset to sunset, in equal parts.

| | |
|---|---|
| First Watch | Sunset to 9 PM |
| Second Watch | 9 PM to Midnight |
| Third Watch | Midnight to 3 AM |
| Fourth Watch | 3 AM to sunrise |

| | |
|---|---|
| First Watch | Sunrise to 9 AM |
| Second Watch | 9 AM to Noon |
| Third Watch | Noon to 3 PM |
| Fourth Watch | 3 PM to sunset |

## Notes – Things I want to remember

_____

_____

_____

_____

_____

_____

_____

_____

_____

# HEBREW DAYS OF THE WEEK

**E**XCEPT FOR THE SABBATH DAY, the individual days of the week have no names, just numbers. The middle column in the table below gives the actual transliterated pronunciation of the names.

**Yom** is pronounced "Yome."

The "Kh" is a guttural sound often spelled as "Ch." There is no "Ch" sound in Hebrew as there is in English. Modern Hebrew, however, can create a "Ch" sound by putting an accent mark ( ´ ) in front of the Hebrew letter "Khet" (or "Chet"). This is used only in rare cases in order to properly pronounce such words or names as Church or Churchill (referring to the person Winston Churchill.)

| Secular Weekday Name | Hebrew "Name" | Hebrew Meaning |
|---|---|---|
| Sunday | Yom Reeshone | First day |
| Monday | Yom Shaynee | Second day |
| Tuesday | Yom Shlee´shee | Third day |
| Wednesday | Yom Revee´ee | Fourth day |
| Thursday | Yom Khah´mee´shee | Fifth day |
| Friday | Yom Shee´shee | Sixth day |
| Saturday | Shabbat | Rest |

# RESOURCES FOR RESEARCH

## First Fruits of Zion

https://torahportions.ffoz.org

- The weekly Torah portion schedule and Torah commentary.

## Hayesod

https://hayesod.ffoz.org

- The HaYesod organization educates believers about their relationship with the promised land and the Jewish historical context of the Scripture.

- Hayesod The Foundation Student Workbook 2010 by Boaz Michael

## 119 Ministries

https://www.119ministries.com

- Excellent analysis of Torah and Christian topics.

## TorahResource

https://www.torahresource.com

- Great Bible study resource that is focused on Yeshua and grounded in Torah.

## Jewels of Judaism

https://www.jewelsofjudaism.com/category/torah-portion

- In-depth Torah portion analysis.

## Jewish Voice

https://www.jewishvoice.org

- Jewish Voice exists to transform lives and see all Israel saved.

## International Christian Embassy, Jerusalem

https://int.icej.org

- Great way to connect with Israel.

## Hebrew for Christians

https://www.hebrew4christians.com

## Jewish Virtual Library

https://www.jewishvirtuallibrary.org

## My Jewish Learning

https://www.myjewishlearning.com

## Times of Israel

https://www.timesofisrael.com
- **Good way to stay informed about Israel.**

## Hebrew Alphabet

https://www.jewfaq.org/hebrew-alphabet

https://www.israelbookshop.com/

## Notes – Things I want to remember

# CONTACT US

**T**HE CREATION OF THIS BOOK WAS A LABOR OF LOVE. We make these materials available to those who hunger for knowledge and understanding and to encourage biblical education.

Son of David Messianic Fellowship can be found on Facebook and YouTube for meeting schedules and live streaming of services and activities at:

http://sonofdavidaz.com

Please consider making donations to this ministry to make gift copies possible to spread the Word. *I Am Newish Jewish* books are available on Amazon and Barnes & Noble. Questions regarding the purchase of multiple copies at a group rate for training purposes, please contact the ministry at:

christine@sonofdavidaz.com or 623.499.2612 voice / text

The above ministry phone number can be used for Zelle donations.

Please make checks payable to:

"Son of David Messianic Fellowship"

Mailing Address:
Son of David Messianic Fellowship
c/o Rev. Julie Caliendo
3324 E. Ray Rd, #646
Higley, AZ 85236

*This is just the beginning...Shalom!*

1. View of the Sea of Galilee with the fish caught that morning for their lunch.
2. Julie at her Bat Mitzvah, May 15, 2021, presenting in English and Hebrew.
3. Caesarea shores from the ruins of King Herod's Palace.
4. Standing atop the Mt. of Olives, I met this man. He pointed to his donkey and called it the Jesus taxi.
5. Grocery shopping at the Shuk Market in Jerusalem.
6. Visiting the Western (Wailing) Wall in Jerusalem I could hear the hum of prayers ascending during Passover week.

# About the Author

**J**ULIE CALIENDO GREW UP ON THE SOUTH side of Chicago attending a Baptist church, but also participated with her family in the Catholic church for special occasions. Her father was one of six brothers, three were Baptist and the other three Catholic. It was a family thing to respect both places of worship. This gave her the ability to view her Christian faith from two perspectives leaving her open to broader horizons ahead. At eleven years old Julie gave her heart to Jesus and was baptized in the Baptist church.

Julie is an ordained minister and has been serving the cause of Christ for over thirty years. In 2019, she was introduced to the pastors of Son of David Messianic Fellowship, a group which would be holding Saturday services at Chandler First Assemblies of God Church, which is where she worshipped. As an avid student of the Bible, she ventured in with open heart and mind to see what they were all about. Through their teaching, she saw the Bible with eyes of discovery. There was so much she didn't understand about the Torah, the feasts, and Old Testament commands of God. Sermon after sermon, she compiled copious notes as part of her methodical learning process. It was as if she was reading the Bible for the first time. Such excitement! Thus, her journey began, with a voracious appetite.

Julie's professional life: She worked for eleven years as an instructional designer in the fraud department for a major credit card company in Phoenix. She wrote training manuals and materials for fraud investigators. She was also a contributing editor for an internal news publication, *Express It*, with a staff of reporters.

As a retiree now, Julie serves the cause of Christ in full time ministry. When her husband died in 2016, she attended a Bible-based, Christ-centered grief recovery program: "GriefShare." After participating in her first series of classes for herself, she started a grief recovery ministry at her church and has been a facilitator and ministry leader ever since helping others overcome their loss of loved ones.

This lady keeps busy with various community organizations: Toastmasters International for over twenty-five years to hone her public speaking and leadership skills, Widow Warriors ministry to support other widows, Mesa Christian Writer's Group to raise the bar on her writing skills.

Clear communication is important to Julie. She is not only a public speaker and author, she served in church as an interpreter for the deaf for many years. She graduated from the Phoenix College Interpreter for the Deaf Training Program and has been involved in Deaf Ministry since 1988. She published her first book: *"A Christian Interpreter's Code of Ethics."* Her goal was to raise a standard and equip church interpreters to serve God in the deaf community.

Julie embraces her Christian faith through participation in two churches, just as she did as a growing child. Once again Julie is bridging a gap between two worlds: Baptist and Catholic, Deaf and hearing lives, Christian and Jewish/biblical beliefs. On Saturdays she is an active member and Elder of Son of David Messianic Fellowship, the inspiration for this book. On Sundays she attends Chandler First Assembly, who hosts the GriefShare ministry. God uses her now to impact both Christian denominations. She is Newish Jewish on Saturdays and Pentecostal on Sundays. What a calling!

# The Stained-Glass Cross Logo

**T**HE DESIGN OF THE STAINED-GLASS CROSS as a logo came to Julie in a vision. She always loved the colorful cuts of glass she saw adorning churches, as well as other structures and works of art. Each had a unique design that created a picture or told a story. When writing her first book, she sought the Lord in prayer about a logo that would give Him the glory. Her mind's eye saw an alluring colorful cross, then He gave her the meaning.

The various hues and tones represented her emotional, as well as spiritual journey through life. The shards symbolized the broken pieces of her past. The colors reflected joys and sorrows, pain and passion, love and laughter, in a magnificent explosion of colors.

Once Julie surrendered her life to the cause of Christ, He transformed her brokenness into the beauty of the stained-glass cross. The white glowing light at the center is symbolic of the purity that was restored to her heart and mind. She was forgiven once and for all time.

May the brilliance of this cross remind you of the broken shards of your past that were forgiven in the ultimate act of love. Julie wrote the following poem decades before this event, but the story still resonates.

# PORTRAIT BY THE MASTER

IF I COULD GIVE SOMEONE A GIFT,
It would be a picture true,
Of themselves and what they're seeking,
Of the things they often do.

IF THEY COULD LOOK UPON A CANVAS
And see their strokes without sense,
No meaning to the figures,
No purpose, so busy, too intense.

I'M SURE THERE'D BE A FRENZY
Of colors splashed to and fro,
Without form or direction
To show where their lives go.

FATHER, I KNOW THAT THEIR CANVAS
Was created with love by you,
That it needs your divine palate
The Master's hand they must pursue.

YOU ARE THE AUTHOR OF THE PAINT
From whom the colors flow,
The brilliance in their lives
Is you Lord, and they should know!

FROM THE VIBRANT REDS AND YELLOWS
To the peaceful greens and blues
They'll find all life's moments
Are expressed by hues.

**MY PRAYER IS TO SHOW THEM A PICTURE**
Of what life could be,
With you as the ultimate artist
Guiding each brushstroke with new reality.

**THEIR PICTURE WOULD HAVE VARIATION**
Some dark tones but mostly light,
Warm colors and also cool ones
Perfect blending for soothing sight.

**UPON EACH PERSON'S COUNTENANCE**
There'd be a glow, as such,
To tell the world their beauty
Comes from the Master's touch.

**OCTOBER 20, 1986**

# Also by Julie Caliendo

**A Christian Interpreter's Code of Ethics Workshop and Self-Study Guide for Church Interpreters for the Deaf and Hard of Hearing, Complete with Facilitator's Guide.**

Published: October 15, 2018
Language: English
Paperback: 102 pages
ISBN-13: 978-1643491523
AVAILABLE AT BARNES & NOBLE AND AMAZON

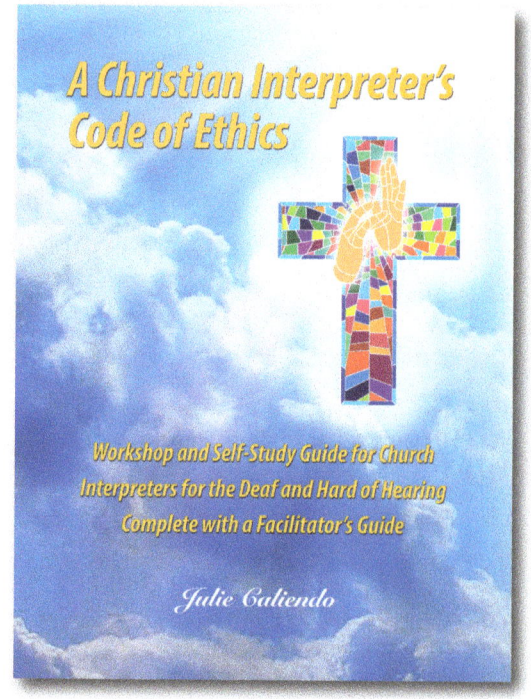

## What's This Book All About?

The *"Christian Interpreter's Code of Ethics"* is about interpreting for the deaf in church settings. It establishes a standard of ethical behavior and a written resource for those who believe God is calling them to participate in Deaf Ministry within Christian churches. It is about behavior and relationships, not the beautiful expressive language of the Deaf. It is a workbook that:

- Presents real-life scenarios to prepare the workers for the everyday life.

- Identifies frequent communication challenges.

- Provides scriptural support to assist decision making including guided prayers.

- Lays a foundation setting expectations for aspiring and tenured interpreters, ministry leaders, pastors, and church staff.

What is stated here has been tried and tested and it works! This is about behavior and relationships, not sign language. This is a guide, not the law. There are many books about starting, managing and growing a Deaf Ministry, but they were more about administration than behavior. The initial goal of this book was and remains: for the learner to better understand the roles and responsibilities as a communication link, perform with increased professionalism, and serve this special calling of God with a committed mind and heart.

www.ingramcontent.com/pod-product-compliance
Lightning Source LLC
Chambersburg PA
CBHW041519120626
46551CB00018B/2498